Finnigin's Bushy Tail

By
Mary Anne Miceli

Art
by Dianne Gagnon Caputo

Author Page

Mary Anne, a North Shore resident, is a Boston native of Irish extraction, who has studied her ancestral roots. Mary Anne has always loved nursery rhymes and music and often composes poetry in 'rhyming rhythm'.

Website: bostonnorthshorestoriesandpoems.com

Published books:
Children Picture Books: *Boston North Shore's Rhyming Fish Tales; Boston North Shore's Salem's Golden Broomstick; Boston North Shore's Teeny, Tiny, Ticks; Boston North Shore's Mouse Tales of Early Salem; Boston North Shore's Tales of Webs; Boston North Shore's Car Wash Squid; China Baby Doll; How 'Pilly-Pine', the Alpaca, Lost his Quills; Confessor's Animal Wartime Blues and Music - Home of Middle C.*

Poetry Books: *Poetry: Reflecting on the Clouds of Everyday Living; Poetry: Aging Ever So Gracefully; Poetry: Everyday Musings and Poetry: Death Chimes.*

Dedication

I dedicate this book to my daughter, Samantha, a gifted artist, who has always shown effort, determination and desire to successfully complete any challenge as well as an innate drive to overcome adversity.

Finnigin's Bushy Tail

Finnigin's bushy tail grows and swells
Wide enough to go down wells …
It grows so long and wide so fast
It scares all OTHER CATS … EVEN RATS!

It can also change its color code
Varying from orange to shiny gold!

These changes can occur in a moment, a flash -
Causing other cats to run off in a dash!

9

For they are fearful of Finnigin's tail
Some - too afraid and some - too frail!

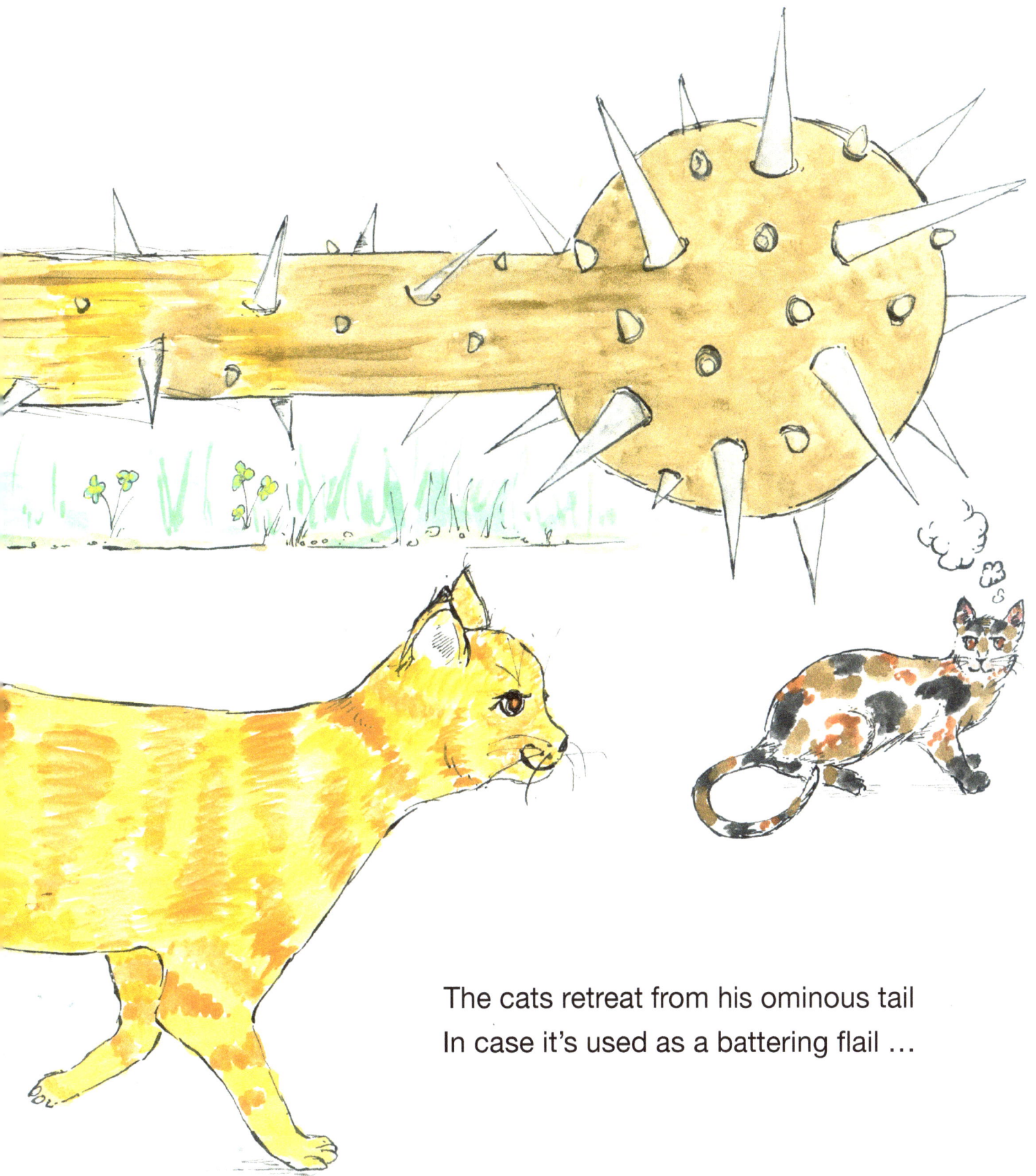

The cats retreat from his ominous tail
In case it's used as a battering flail …

For Finnigin swings his tail straight out
Knocking everything all about …
His tail becomes a BATTLE WEAPON
Should he encounter any rejection!

Including, missing a meal on time
Or, breaking a toy or losing a dime!

For, Finnigin does not accept frustration very well
So, his tail just SWELLS and SWELLS!!!
To the surprise of all around -
His growing tail knows NO BOUNDS!

So his owners devise a plan
To help Finnigin understand -

How to be patient and contemplate
Before losing his temper with his playmates,
Letting him be in control -
To watch his anger, calm his soul!

So, his owners blind Finnigin with a black mask
Making it hard for him to complete any task …

For Finnigin needs to control his own fate
Before he frightens and loses all his playmates!

Soon, Finnigin knocks into chairs and tables
Learning how it feels to be hurt and unable …

So, his questions of where he can now go –
Just grow **and grow and grow!**

To know where to go?
Or, where to lie low?
To know where to nap?
Or, where not to catnap?

As he has no inkling of just where he may be -
He must use his tail to navigate every degree:
From whence he is coming
To where he is going!
Finnigin's tail, now a navigational tool -
No longer makes him a tempestuous fool!

His once bushy tail now sways only at rest
Providing him peace in a world full of pets -
Without lingering duress
And no more regrets!!
No longer so long or so wide
His bushy tail's swelling subsides -
Back to its normal color and size.

No longer a threat to any cat - or rat
Finnigin's tail no longer fights back –

For, he's as tame and mellow as can be
No longer needing the mask which helped set him free!

www.ingramcontent.com/pod-product-compliance
Lightning Source LLC
Chambersburg PA
CBHW061237270326
41930CB00023B/3494